Working in Canadian Communities
JOBS IN CANADIAN CITIES

TRUE NORTH

BY DIANE BAILEY

True North is published by Beech Street Books
27 Stewart Rd. Collingwood, ON Canada L9Y 4M7

www.beechstreetbooks.ca

Produced by Red Line Editorial

Photographs ©: Volodymyr Kyrylyuk/iStockphoto/Thinkstock, cover, 1; Chutima Chaochaiya/Shutterstock Images, 4–5; gmlykin/Shutterstock Images, 6–7; mikecphoto/Shutterstock Images, 8–9; Anya Ivanova/Shutterstock Images, 10–11; Paul McKinnon/Shutterstock Images, 12–13; Ryan Hutchinson/Shutterstock Images, 14; CandyBox Images/Shutterstock Images, 16–17; Monkey Business Images/Shutterstock Images, 18–19; Red Line Editorial, 20–21

Editor: Heather C. Hudak
Designer: Laura Polzin

Library and Archives Canada Cataloguing in Publication

Bailey, Diane, 1966-, author
    Jobs in Canadian cities / by Diane Bailey.

(Working in Canadian communities)
Includes bibliographical references and index.
Issued in print and electronic formats.
ISBN 978-1-77308-024-6 (hardback).--ISBN 978-1-77308-052-9 (paperback).--
ISBN 978-1-77308-080-2 (pdf).--ISBN 978-1-77308-108-3 (html)

    1. Occupations--Canada--Juvenile literature. 2. Cities and towns--
Canada--Juvenile literature. 3. City and town life--Canada--Juvenile
literature. I. Title.

HF5382.5.C2B35 2016   j331.700971   C2016-903598-0
                                              C2016-903599-9

Printed in the United States of America
Mankato, MN
August 2016

TABLE OF CONTENTS

Chapter One

GET IT, GROW IT, MAKE IT!

A city is a busy place. Approximately two out of three Canadians live in a city. They have a lot of different jobs. They help the city run.

Canada has many **natural resources**. These are things that come from the earth. There is gold in Ontario and salt in Saskatchewan. Forests in British Columbia are full of wood. Oil is another important natural resource. It is used to make gasoline for cars. It is also used to heat homes.

Oil comes from deep under the ground. Geologists are scientists who study the earth. They must find the oil. **Engineers** look for ways to dig out the oil. It is a big job! These scientists do some of their work in a **laboratory**.

There are more than 73,000 engineers and geologists in Alberta.

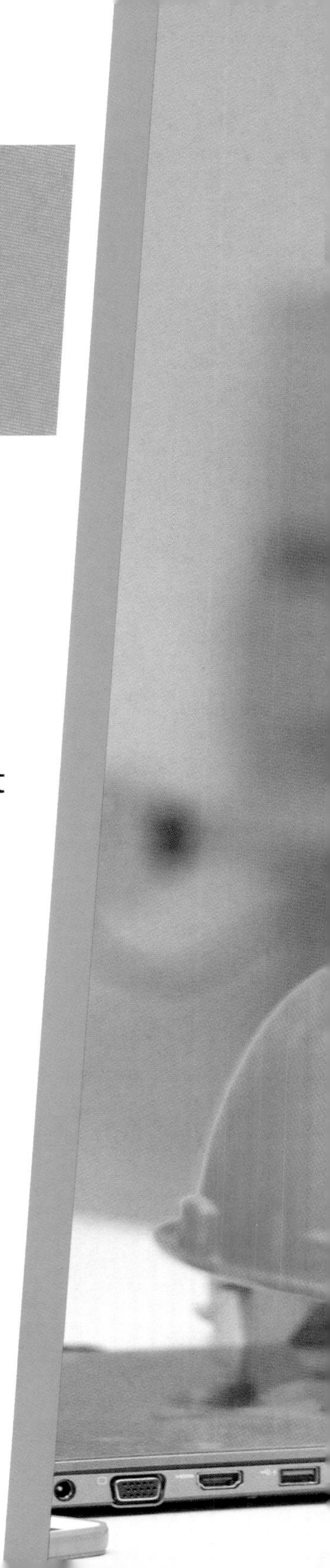

It has special tools for them to use. Calgary, Alberta, is a city that has many laboratories.

Food is another big industry in Canada. Farmers in Saskatchewan and Manitoba grow crops, such as wheat. Milk comes from cows raised in Quebec and Ontario. Then these products go to a **factory**. There are factories in cities like Toronto and Winnipeg. In factories workers make the wheat into flour and bread. They put the milk into cartons or bags. Now, the food is ready to go to the grocery store.

Canada also produces many products. Workers make cars in Oshawa and Windsor, Ontario. They make clothing in Winnipeg. They make clocks in Ottawa.

BUILDING AN AIRPLANE

More than 80,000 Canadians build and design aircraft. This industry is called aerospace. Many people in Montreal build airplanes. An airplane will not fit into a normal room. Workers need a lot of space to build one. They work in huge rooms called hangars. These rooms can hold a whole plane.

Most factories are huge buildings. They have many large machines inside. This machine is used to bottle milk.

7

Chapter Two

GET MOVING

Products made in one part of Canada are sent to other parts of the country. Some are even sent to other parts of the world. Transportation is a big business.

People at factories put products in boxes and crates. They load them onto trucks and trains. Truck drivers drive on the Trans-Canada highway. The country also has thousands of kilometres of railroad tracks.

Sometimes containers go on a ship. The ships wait in a port. A port is on the water. There are large ports in Vancouver and Montreal.

People in transport often lift heavy boxes. They may work late nights. They work outside in all weather.

GO Trains connect cities across southern Ontario.

PEOPLE MOVERS

People need to move from one place to the next. In the city, they can ride a bus or take a train. In some cities, the trains are above ground. In other places, they are in tunnels underground. This is called a subway. Train and bus drivers take people to stops and stations. These are found all over the city. People in Toronto and Ottawa use **mass transit** a lot. In those cities, the average person takes more than 100 trips per year.

Chapter Three

NEW IDEAS

Have you ever talked on a cell phone? Do you like to use a computer? You are using high **technology**. You can say "high tech" for short! High-tech workers make computers. They make machines to help sick people. They make cars that do not need gasoline.

High-tech workers come up with new ideas. They do a lot of research. They find out how things work.

There are many high-tech companies in Canada. In Winnipeg people make medicine and medical devices. Workers in Toronto and Waterloo make communication equipment. High-tech workers do their jobs in laboratories and offices. They may work at universities.

More than 800,000 Canadians work in computer technology.

VIDEO GAMES

Software tells a computer what to do. Many workers in Vancouver write software for video games. Canada produces the third-most video games of any country in the world. There are more than 170 video game companies in Vancouver alone.

Chapter Four

HAVE FUN!

There are fun things to do in a city. You can listen to people play music. You can look at art. You can watch dancers in a park. A city is full of **culture**. It is all around you!

Actors, dancers, artists, and musicians are all creative people. Many of them live in cities. They can work with other artists. They can get ideas from each other. They can also show their work to other people. Many visitors come to Canadian cities. They want to experience the culture.

Aboriginal Peoples have their own customs, food, and clothes, depending on where they live in Canada. Their cultures have special music and dances.

The Summer Solstice Aboriginal Arts Festival is held in Ottawa, Ontario.

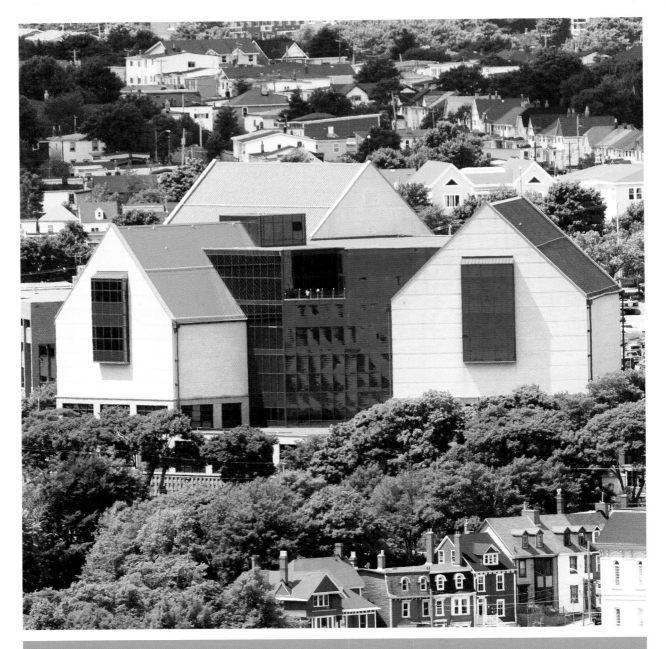

The Rooms in St. John's, Newfoundland and Labrador, is home to the provincial museum, art gallery, and archives.

Many communities celebrate their culture at powwows. There, people perform traditional dances and music. Powwows are held in many Canadian cities. Thousands of people attend. Winnipeg, Edmonton, Vancouver, Toronto, and Calgary have a large population of Aboriginal people.

Most cities in Canada have art museums and galleries. Here, you can view artwork. A lot of the art is made by people who live in Canada. There are many paintings, photographs, and sculptures. The National Gallery of Canada is a museum in Ottawa. It has many paintings by Aboriginal people.

A lot of people in Vancouver make movies. There are many buildings and parks. There are also many shops and streets. People can film a movie in many different places. There are a lot of places to choose from. *The Lightning Thief*, *Man of Steel*, and *Tomorrowland* are some movies that were made in Vancouver.

Chapter Five

HELPING OUT

Everybody needs help sometimes. Most people in Canada work in **service**, while other people volunteer. They do things to help other people.

Maybe you do not feel well. Then you go to the doctor. Doctors know how to take care of sick people. They give you medicine to make you feel better. Sometimes people need an operation. Then they go to a hospital. There are big hospitals in cities throughout Canada.

Bus drivers take people to work and school. They go all over the city. A mail carrier brings letters and packages to your neighbourhood. At the store, a checkout clerk rings up your groceries. Maybe you go out to dinner at

Dentists help treat and prevent mouth diseases.

INQUIRY QUESTIONS

Why do people live in cities? Why are some types of jobs located there?

a restaurant. A waiter takes your order. A cook makes your food.

Teachers help you learn things. They show you how to read and do math. Teachers work at schools and colleges. There are about five million children in Canada's schools. There need to be a lot of teachers to help them all!

Some people work in trades. They have special skills. If the kitchen sink is broken, a plumber comes to fix it. If the lights do not work, you can call an electrician for help. Carpenters build houses for people to live in. They build tall skyscrapers where people work. Construction is an important business in Vancouver. The city keeps growing!

RUNNING THE COUNTRY

Canada is a big country. Many people help run it. They work for the **government**. Each city has its own government. The person in charge is the mayor. Canada also has a national government. It is for all of Canada. It is in Ottawa. This is the nation's capital. Nearly 430,000 people work for the national government.

There are more than 750,000 teachers and professors in Canada.

19

WHAT A CITY LOOKS LIKE

DOWNTOWN

PLAYGROUND

AIRPORT

MARKET

NEIGHBOURHOOD

GAS

APARTMENTS

POLICE

GAS

SUPERMARKET

SHOP

COFFEE

Burger

TRAIN

1 CM = 0.5 KM
— = ROUTE TO WORK

N
W ◆ E
S

20

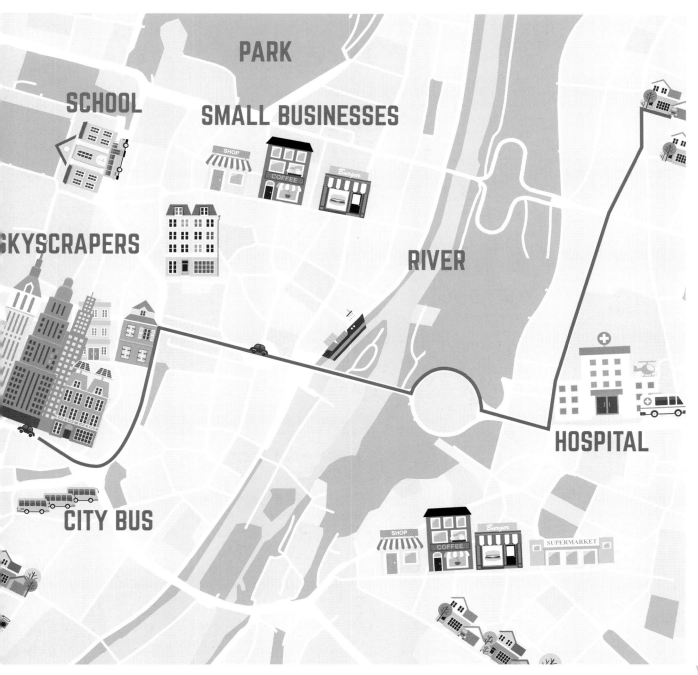

PARK

SCHOOL

SMALL BUSINESSES

SHOP

COFFEE

Burger

SKYSCRAPERS

RIVER

CITY BUS

HOSPITAL

SHOP

COFFEE

Burger

SUPERMARKET

21

GLOSSARY

CULTURE
the customs and traditions of a group of people

ENGINEERS
scientists trained to design machines, buildings, and other structures or systems

FACTORY
a place where many people work to make products

GALLERIES
places that display art

GOVERNMENT
the people and laws that make a country run

LABORATORY
a place with lots of equipment where scientists work

MASS TRANSIT
public transportation that carries many people at the same time

NATURAL RESOURCES
things that come from the earth, such as oil or wood

PORT
a place on water where ships come in and out

SERVICE
something that someone does to help someone else

SOFTWARE
a kind of technology that makes computers work

TECHNOLOGY
the use of science to make new things

TRANSPORTATION
the act of moving people and products around, using vehicles such as cars, trains, planes, and ships

TO LEARN MORE

BOOKS

Bowers, Vivien. *Wow Canada! Exploring This Land from Coast to Coast to Coast*. Toronto: Owlkids Books, 2010.

Gürth, Per-Henrik. *ABC of Toronto*. Toronto: Kids Can Press, 2013.

Juarez, Christine. *Canada*. Mankato, MN: Capstone Press, 2013.

WEBSITES

THE CANADA ATLAS ONLINE
www.canadiangeographic.ca/atlas/intro.aspx?lang=En#

CANADIAN GEOGRAPHIC GAMES
www.canadiangeographic.ca/kids/games/default.asp

KIDPORT
www.kidport.com/reflib/worldgeography/canada/Canada.htm

KIDS WORLD TRAVEL GUIDE
www.kids-world-travel-guide.com/canada-facts-for-kids.html

INDEX

ABOUT THE AUTHOR

Diane Bailey has written nearly 50 nonfiction books for kids and teens. She also works as a freelance editor, helping authors who write novels for children and young adults. Diane has two sons and two dogs.